T0193340

Gardening
by the Silvery Moon
APRIL 2018—MARCH 2019

HELEN KOLADA

BALBOA.
PRESS

A DIVISION OF HAY HOUSE

Balboa Press books may be ordered through booksellers or by contacting:

Balboa Press
A Division of Hay House
1663 Liberty Drive
Bloomington, IN 47403
www.balboapress.com
1 (877) 407-4847

Print information available on the last page.

ISBN: 978-1-9822-0260-6 (sc)
ISBN: 978-1-9822-0261-3 (e)

Library of Congress Control Number: 2018905039

Balboa Press rev. date: 04/26/2018

Foreword

It was my mother who opened the door to influence me, a little 6 year old girl, to share her love of flower gardening and my grandmother to inspire my love of vegetable gardening. My parents both grew up in Belarus and gardening was part of their everyday life, just like their parents. My father's job as a little boy was to tend the 40 beehives the family raised for money. Gardening is seeded deep within my DNA. I love to garden, and marvel at the mystery and magic of watching a tiny little seed grow to something mature and magnificent. It has always been a fascination of mine to witness this act of nature. This book is not going to address  what man has done over the last 50 years to genetically modify crops or how the chemicals we put on our plants and into our soil have disrupted the balance of nature. Healthy living is becoming more and more of a mainstream priority of conscious living today. Healthy living is about healthy balance on many levels. Starting with the physical body, what you eat is what your physical body absorbs. A way to begin to get back in balance with nature is to start growing your own foods or eating organic foods when possible. You wouldn't be reading this book if you were not interested in a balanced way of life. Exploring and embracing gardening by the moon is a step towards a more balanced life in general.

Growing up in America, I was raised by my parents and grandparents in the ways of the "old country". In the early 60's, as most American's began to consume TV dinners as the first expression of fast food, we shopped at the Cleveland West Side Market where local farmers sold their produce. At the West Side Market, you would see live chickens running around. We picked our chicken and the butcher did the rest. I can remember when my grandfather butchered a pig in our basement. That was the way of life of someone who was born in Europe. Times were different then. My grandmother always had a vegetable garden and my mother always had a huge flower garden with many different varieties. It was the way of life for them. As a 6 year old little girl, I would pull weeds with my mother; it was our way of bonding.

Between the 5th grade and 6th grade, "summer school" was comprised of working in a community garden in the Cleveland public school system. Planting, pulling weeds with like-minded children became a fun way to spend the summer. We then brought our share of the harvest home in the fall.

When I moved into my own home at the age of 22, I began a vegetable and flower garden and have gardened ever since.

25 years later, I decided to take gardening to another level. I was inspired by my teacher, Martha C. Mordecai, to embrace gardening techniques by following natures' cycles. For me, that opened the door to explore gardening by the moon. After studying metaphysics for 36 years, I found myself wanting to express what has enriched my life and help others to re-connect with a part of their spirit through nature; a spirit that has been lost, forgotten or buried deep inside their psychic and physical bodies.

As you embark in the practice of gardening by the moon, take it one step at a time. Over years of trials, I have explored the techniques discussed in this book, Enjoy the journey of finding out how our ancestors followed the moon cycles to garden. Uncover your roots as you explore.

Contents

Acknowledgements

Creating a book is a life long journey, even if it has only been the last year of actual writing. As I look back to see how I have arrived to this point and who has been a part of this journey, I found many mentors throughout my life. You can't write a book without having a love and a passion for the subject and I appreciate the love of gardening which was inspired by my Mother and her Mother, my Grandmother.

This project was inspired by my Teacher, Martha C. Mordecai who showed me the way to strive and push through obstacles to make this book a reality for which I am truly grateful. The artwork, created for this book, is Zentangle inspired. Judy Montgomery taught me how to draw and relax using the principle of Zentangle. No book is complete without editing and Kim T. Segebarth helped to make this book readable, or "user friendly. They say you can't tell a book by its cover, but in this case, the cover does give the feeling of the book. The design of the moon is mine, but the coloring, shading and cover design is created by Lenny Kolada who truly has patience when it counts for which I give many thanks.

It is said that "it takes a village" and this project proves that statement. I am truly grateful for those who are in my life who radiate positivity and those who have been a mentor to me throughout my life.

Introduction

Do what you love and the energy will follow. Martha C. Mordecai

Gardening by the moon has been practiced for ages. There is evidence that the Egyptian and Babylonian cultures practiced the art of lunar cycles during gardening activities. In the 1800's, the "*The Old Farmer's Almanac*" acknowledged the rising and setting of the sun, the tides and the weather. It was the most popular of the two almanacs available at the time, the other being *Poor Richard's Almanack* published in 1739 by Richard Saunders, the pseudonym of Benjamin Franklin. One of the reasons Benjamin Franklin created *The Farmers Almanac* was to give information to the farmers to assist in planting by the moon cycle. The old saying "planting by the light of the moon" refers to the phases of the moons. The Almanac included weather forecasts, practical household hints, puzzles and other amusements. The "*Old Farmer's Almanac*" is still published today. Looking at the Almanacs on the news stands today, you can identify the original version by a hole drilled in the upper left hand corner of the book. Back in the 1800's, each book was drilled with a hole so it was hung, for easy reference, from a nail in the barn. Both publications used the cycle of the moon to suggest when to plant.

During the moon's 28-day cycle, the moon passes through each of the twelve zodiac signs. The moon is in each sign two to three days. Each sign of the zodiac is associated with one of the elements: earth, air, water and fire. And as you see in the illustration that follows, each sign is also associated with a body part. This image appeared in the 1800's and is still published in every *Old Farmer's Almanac* today.

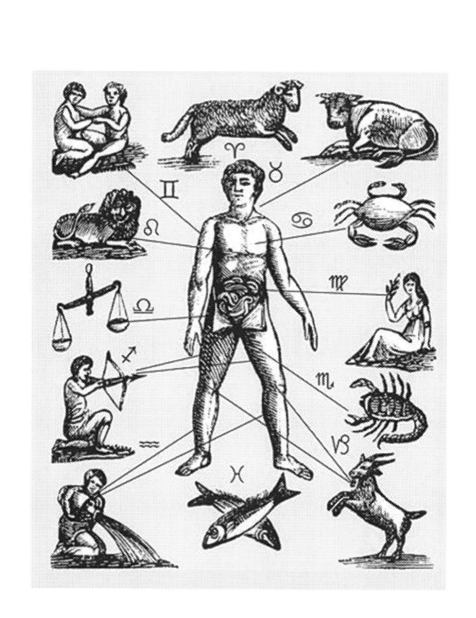

As we will see in the following chapters, some signs are conducive to planting, others for destroying weeds or harvesting. Later we will discuss how the moon's gravitational pull has been scientifically proven to affect the tides, the plants and the soil. Just as planting by moon cycles creates favorable conditions for growing, moon cycles also determine the most favorable times to destroy weeds or harvest crops.

Rudolf Steiner (1861-1925), an Austrian scientist, philosopher and biodynamic agriculturalist, believed humanity would destroy the earth if it did not begin to develop a harmonious relationship with the spirit and physical worlds. Steiner was the first voice at the turn of the last century to point out the dangers of the chemicals being used in farming. His efforts have been named "biodynamic gardening". The Prince of Wales, an advocate of organic farming, embraced biodynamic planting seeds according to phases of the moon. Steiner also taught the importance of following nature's cycles for optimal production. He believed if you used chemical fertilizers, you "forced" water into a plant which caused disease of the plant and fruit.

Our ancestors have known for millennium how the unseen force of the moon affect our lives. Scientists today have proven the phases of the moon affect the tides of the oceans. We watch as ground water, the oceans and the water tables rise during the full moon. Have you considered the sap of a plant rises during the full moon? Esoteric tradition teaches us to avoid surgery of any kind during the full moon as that time arouses excess bleeding. If you were to prune your plant or a tree during the full moon, you would induce bleeding of the sap. The flow of our blood works much the same as the sap of a plant.

Planting by the moon cannot be a rigid science; you will quickly learn to be flexible as well. If the skies pour rain for days or weeks and the planting by the moon is in two weeks, do you plant now while it rains or wait two weeks? When following the cycles of the moon, you must also be practical.

Uncovering that which has been lost

Life begins the day you start a garden. Chinese proverb

Some things to consider …
Fifty years ago, in a city where the land was dry and barren and only grew brush, a group of Scottish people embarked on The Findhorn Project with a goal of growing vegetation on the barren land. Their plan was to work with the nature spirits and angelic kingdom to grow on this land that which was never grown before. They became famous for growing a 42 pound cabbage. Those who worked on the Findhorn project established a relationship with the plants themselves. They believed plants had a relationship with the nature spirits, sometimes called the devic kingdom.

During George Washington's first term as President, Robert B. Thomas published important information for the farmer in *The Farmer's Almanac* which included the rising and setting of the Sun, the tides and the weather.

- Hippocrates, 400 BC, in addition to being a philosopher, was an astrologer.
- Aristotle, 384 BC, Greek philosopher and scientist was an astrologer.
- In the 1500's, a medical doctor was required to be educated as an astrologer.

Following the lead of the church, by 1650, public opinion turned against astrology. Those who practiced and followed astrology went underground. Therefore, by the 1700's, astrologers were hard to find.

1

It wasn't until the 1960's that we saw the "re-birth" of astrology into mainstream America.

You can practice gardening by the moon cycle without being an astrologer but understand that gardening by the moon has its foundation in astrological cycles.

"Scientific Approach"

We can complain because rose bushes have thorns, or rejoice because thorn bushes have roses. Abraham Lincoln

Research has shown planting seeds two days before a full moon is an excellent time to sow seeds and this is where I began my experience of gardening by the moon. 10 years ago, I took all that I had learned about moon cycles to the test. I prepared two soil beds in 5 foot lengths in my garden. I calculated the best time to plant a tomato plant and bought 2 tomato plants that looked identical. I planted the first one in what the books said was an ideal time and planted the second plant on an "unfavorable" day. Then I watched them grow.

As I would have expected, the plant that was planted during a favorable moon cycle grew taller, stronger and healthier. I continued to give them the same amount of love, water and fertilizer. The tomato planted during the favorable time also produced more tomatoes with a sweeter flavor than the other.

I have replicated the experiment with flower seeds and other plants. Every time I saw the same results. Planting during a favorable time produced stronger, healthier and tastier produce.

Today, I don't do any gardening without referencing the moon's planting calendar. To continue my journey, I have embraced "companion planting" which I will discuss later.

Basic facts about the moon

Gardening teaches us the fundamentals in care and the evolution of living things, all while inspiring us to nurture our minds and to relax and strengthen our bodies. Melania Trump

The moon travels around the earth approximately every 28 days. Dividing 28 days by four gives us 4 phases of seven days each.

- New Moon (1st Quarter)
- 2nd Quarter
- Full Moon (3rd Quarter)
- 4th Quarter

New Moon –This is the beginning of the "waxing" period. The gravitational pull of the moon draws water in an upward motion. Planting at this time creates a balance between the leaves of the plants and the roots.

2nd Quarter Moon – To a lesser degree, the moon is still waxing, drawing water in an upward motion. Planting during this phase promotes strong leaf growth.

Full Moon / 3rd Quarter Moon – At the time of the full moon, the gravitational pull is strong which creates moisture in the soil. As the

Did you Know
It takes 28 days for a duck or turkey to hatch from an egg?

Did you Know
Skin, creates a new layer of skin every 28 days?

Did you Know
Cutting hair during the waxing moon stimulates growth of the hair.

Therefore, cutting hair during a waning moon slows down the growth, so, you can cut less often. When hair is short and you want to go to the stylist less often, cut your hair during a waning moon. Try it and watch it work!

Cut your hair during a waxing moon and watch it grow … fast.

moon begins to wane, there is a decrease of the gravitational pull of the moon and at the same time, the light of the moon also decreases. This is a good time to plant root plant including bulbs where the energy is concentrated in the roots.

> **Did you Know**
> Cutting grass during the waxing moon stimulates growth of the grass. Mowing grass during a waning moon slows down the growth so you cut less often.

4th Quarter Moon - During this period, it is considered a "resting" period. The gravitational pull is diminished and the light of the moon is decreased. The water tables are at their lowest. This is a good time to harvest, cultivate, transplant and weed. Tides are the highest at the new and full moon – therefore moisture is rising.

Important keys for gardening by the moon.

- The moon has 4 phases lasting approximately 7 days each.
- The 1st two quarters of the moon phase are waxing – which is increasing in light.
- The 3rd and 4th quarters of the moon phase are waning – which is decreasing in light.
- The Earth is covered by 71% water and is influenced by the gravitational pull of the moon.
- Tides are highest at the time of the full moon.

When the moon is full, water from the earth is pulled up through the soil promoting growth. Scientific evidence has shown that seeds will absorb more water during the time of the full moon. Tides also work on sap, which further shows the importance of planting in cycles, even with potted plants.

Unseen Forces

Human beings, vegetables, or cosmic dust, we all dance to a mysterious tune intoned in the distance by an invisible player. Albert Einstein

Have you ever thought about gravity, the force that holds you down on earth? In the 1600's, Sir Isaac Newton, a mathematician, astronomer and physicist formulated the law of gravity inspired by watching an apple fall from a tree. This observation led Newton to mathematically calculate the elliptical paths of the celestial bodies and publish the "three laws of motion and the law of universal gravity".

Now, in your imagination, take yourself back in time to the mid 1800's where there are no telephones, wireless capabilities or electricity. What if, in the 1800's you were told that within 100 years, the following would be available to most everyone?:

- TV programs, including live programming
- Radio waves – live and recorded
- Electricity
- Internet
- Wireless; Bluetooth
- Telegraph (we see that as "ancient" today)
- Telephone – landlines – cell phones

It is mind boggling to think of what progress has transpired, just in our lifetime. If you put yourself back in the mid 1800's, and told someone that all the above would be common for everyone in just 100 years, you would have either been laughed at or put in the "loony bin". Albert Einstein at the age of five was given a compass. He was mystified that an unseen force could influence the movement of the needle. That led him to a lifelong pursuit of unseen forces.

The Moon is only one part of the celestial sphere. Let's not forget the rest of the cast of characters. Their "Unseen" forces also have an effect. But that is discussion for another book.

Let's dip our toes into the subject of astrology for a moment. What? The moment of your birth creates a matrix of the planets that gives a picture of a blueprint that is the foundation of your life. Astrology teaches us that each planet emits a force of energy of a particular quality. Our ancestors studied the ancient art of astrology. In the 900 AD, Ptolemy wrote books on astrology that are still relevant still today.

I believe there are beings that work with us from the angelic or devic kingdoms in the 4th dimension. I have come to learn the benefits when transplanting a plant to ask the devas and, the fairies to let go and prepare themselves for a new home. This helps bring harmony to the plant and the plant will grow stronger.

Working in the garden is a best time for meditation, being in harmony with nature. Anyone can meditate using a prescribed posture with legs crossed and fingertips together. There is a time and place for meditating in that manner. Now consider, a "living" meditation where in the process of gardening, in the process of pulling weeds, you focus your total awareness and attention on the plant, the weed and soil right in front of you. Staying in the present moment is the art of meditation. Being one with nature is feeling the soil, listening to the birds or crickets. If you stay present and listen carefully, the plants will tell you what they need. The art of mindfulness begins in the present moment.

Astrological Signs

"We are born at a given moment, in a given place and, like vintage years of wine, we have the qualities of the year and of the season of which we are born. Astrology does not lay claim to anything more." Carl Jung

Astrological signs of the zodiac correspond with the elements of WATER, EARTH, FIRE and AIR. Each gardening activity is compatible with one of these four elements.

EARTH
- Taurus
- Virgo
- Capricorn

FIRE
- Aries
- Leo
- Sagittarius

WATER
- Cancer
- Scorpio
- Pisces

AIR
- Libra
- Gemini
- Aquarius

Rule of thumb to Follow

Water signs are good for planting leafy vegetables
Earth signs are good for planting root crops
Air signs are good for planting blooming flowers – especially sign of Libra
Fire signs are good for crops grown for seeds

SIGN of:

Aries – Destroy weeds
Taurus – Transplant; prune to LIMIT growth
Gemini – Harvest herbs & root crops
Cancer – Prune to encourage growth
Leo – Prune to shape
Virgo – Till, cultivate, turn compost
Libra – Plant annual flowers, vines, flowers picked will last longest
Scorpio – Prune to encourage growth
Sagittarius – Best sign to harvest crops for maximum storage qualities
Capricorn – Plant bulbs
Aquarius – Harvest crops for long term storage
Pisces – Transplant for vigorous root growth; fertilize

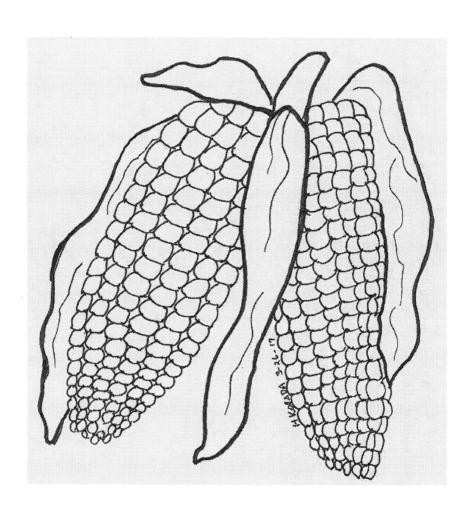

March 2018

Sun	Mon	Tue	Wed	Thu	Fri	Sat
				1 FULL MOON NO GARDENING	**2** Plant Root Crops Till – Cultivate Turn Compost	**3** Plant Flowering Plants Plant Annual Flowers & Vines *Flowers picked will last the longest*
3 Plant Flowering Plants Plant Annual Flowers & Vines *Flowers picked will last the longest*	**5** Plant Leafy Greens Prune to Encourage Growth	**6** Plant Leafy Greens Prune to Encourage Growth	**7** Plant Leafy Greens Prune to Encourage Growth	**8** Plant Fruiting Crops Harvest Crops for Maximum Storage	**9** Weeding & Harvesting Harvest Crops for Maximum Storage	**10** Weeding & Harvesting Plant Bulbs
11 Weeding & Harvesting Plant Bulbs	**12** Weeding & Harvesting Plant Bulbs	**13** Weeding & Harvesting Harvest Crops for Maximum Storage	**14** Weeding & Harvesting Harvest Crops for Maximum Storage	**15** Weeding & Harvesting Transplant for Vigorous Root Growth	**16** Weeding & Harvesting Transplant for Vigorous Root Growth	**17** NEW MOON NO GARDENING

March 2018

Sun	Mon	Tue	Wed	Thu	Fri	Sat
18 Plant Fruiting Crops / Destroy Weeds	**19** Plant Fruiting Crops / Destroy Weeds	**20** Plant Root Crops / Transplant / Prune to Limit Growth	**21** Plant Root Crops / Transplant / Prune to Limit Growth	**22** Plant Flowering Plants / Harvest Herbs & Root Crops	**23** Plant Flowering Plants / Harvest Herbs & Root Crops	**24** Plant Leafy Greens / Prune to Encourage Growth
25 Plant Leafy Greens / Prune to Encourage Growth	**26** Plant Fruiting Crops / Prune to Shape	**27** Plant Fruiting Crops / Prune to Shape	**28** Plant Root Crops / Till – Cultivate Turn Compost	**29** Plant Root Crops / Till – Cultivate Turn Compost	**30** Plant Root Crops / Till – Cultivate Turn Compost	**31** FULL MOON / NO GARDENING

April 2018

Sun	Mon	Tue	Wed	Thu	Fri	Sat
1 Plant Flowering Plants Prune to Encourage Growth	**2** Plant Flowering Plants Prune to Encourage Growth	**3** Plant Flowering Plants Prune to Encourage Growth	**4** Plant Fruiting Crops Harvest Crops for Maximum Storage	**5** Plant Fruiting Crops Harvest Crops for Maximum Storage	**6** Plant Fruiting Crops Plant Bulbs	**7** Plant Root Crops Plant Bulbs
8 Weeding & Harvesting Plant Bulbs	**9** Weeding & Harvesting Harvest Crops for Maximum Storage	**10** Weeding & Harvesting Harvest Crops for Maximum Storage	**11** Weeding & Harvesting Harvest Crops for Maximum Storage	**12** Weeding & Harvesting Transplant for Vigorous Root Growth	**13** Weeding & Harvesting Transplant for Vigorous Root Growth	**14** Weeding & Harvesting Destroy Weeds
15 NEW MOON NO GARDENING	**16** Plant Root Crops Transplant Prune to Limit Growth	**17** Plant Root Crops Transplant Prune to Limit Growth	**18** Plant Flowering Plants Harvest Herbs & Root Crops	**19** Plant Flowering Plants Harvest Herbs & Root Crops	**20** Plant Leafy Greens Prune to Encourage Growth	**21** Plant Leafy Greens Prune to Encourage Growth

April 2018

Sun	Mon	Tue	Wed	Thu	Fri	Sat
22 Plant Leafy Greens Prune to Encourage Growth	**23** Plant Fruiting Crops Prune to Shape	**24** Plant Fruiting Crops Prune to Shape	**25** Plant Root Crops Till – Cultivate Turn Compost	**26** Plant Root Crops Till – Cultivate Turn Compost	**27** Plant Flowering Plants Plant Annual Flowers & Vines *Flowers picked will last the longest*	**28** Plant Flowering Plants Plant Annual Flowers & Vines *Flowers picked will last the longest*
29 FULL MOON NO GARDENING	**30** Plant Leafy Greens Prune to Encourage Growth					

May 2018

Sun	Mon	Tue	Wed	Thu	Fri	Sat
		1 Plant Fruiting Crops / Prune to Encourage Growth	**2** Plant Fruiting Crops / Harvest Crops for Maximum Storage	**3** Plant Fruiting Crops / Harvest Crops for Maximum Storage	**4** Plant Root Crops / Plant Bulbs	**5** Plant Root Crops / Plant Bulbs
6 Plant Flowering Plants / Harvest Crops for Maximum Storage	**7** Weeding & Harvesting / Harvest Crops for Maximum Storage	**8** Weeding & Harvesting / Harvest Crops for Maximum Storage	**9** Weeding & Harvesting / Transplant for Vigorous Root Growth	**10** Weeding & Harvesting / Transplant for Vigorous Root Growth	**11** Weeding & Harvesting / Destroy Weeds	**12** Weeding & Harvesting / Destroy Weeds
13 Weeding & Harvesting / Destroy Weeds	**14** Weeding & Harvesting / Transplant / Prune to Limit Growth	**15** NEW MOON / NO GARDENING	**16** Plant Flowering Plants / Harvest Herbs & Root Crops	**17** Plant Flowering Plants / Harvest Herbs & Root Crops	**18** Plant Leafy Greens / Prune to Encourage Growth	**19** Plant Leafy Greens / Prune to Encourage Growth

May 2018

Sun	Mon	Tue	Wed	Thu	Fri	Sat
20 Plant Fruiting Crops Prune to Shape	**21** Plant Fruiting Crops Prune to Shape	**22** Plant Root Crops Till – Cultivate Turn Compost	**23** Plant Root Crops Till – Cultivate Turn Compost	**24** Plant Flowering Plants Plant Annual Flowers & Vines *Flowers picked will last the longest*	**25** Plant Flowering Plants Plant Annual Flowers & Vines *Flowers picked will last the longest*	**26** Plant Leafy Greens Prune to Encourage Growth
27 Plant Leafy Greens Prune to Encourage Growth	**28** Plant Leafy Greens Prune to Encourage Growth	**29** FULL MOON NO GARDENING	**30** Plant Fruiting Crops Harvest Crops for Maximum Storage	**31** Plant Root Crops Plant Bulbs		

June 2018

Sun	Mon	Tue	Wed	Thu	Fri	Sat
					1 Plant Root Crops / Plant Bulbs	**2** Plant Root Crops / Plant Bulbs
3 Plant Flowering Plants / Harvest Crops for Maximum Storage	**4** Plant Flowering Plants / Harvest Crops for Maximum Storage	**5** Weeding & Harvesting / Transplant for Vigorous Root Growth	**6** Weeding & Harvesting / Transplant for Vigorous Root Growth	**7** Weeding & Harvesting / Transplant for Vigorous Root Growth	**8** Weeding & Harvesting / Destroy Weeds	**9** Weeding & Harvesting / Destroy Weeds
10 Weeding & Harvesting / Transplant / Prune to Limit Growth	**11** Weeding & Harvesting / Transplant / Prune to Limit Growth	**12** Weeding & Harvesting / Harvest Herbs & Root Crops	**13** NEW MOON / NO GARDENING	**14** Plant Leafy Greens / Prune to Encourage Growth	**15** Plant Leafy Greens / Prune to Encourage Growth	**16** Plant Fruiting Crops / Prune to Shape

June 2018

Sun	Mon	Tue	Wed	Thu	Fri	Sat
17 Plant Fruiting Crops Prune to Shape	**18** Plant Root Crops Till – Cultivate Turn Compost	**19** Plant Root Crops Till – Cultivate Turn Compost	**20** Plant Flowering Plants Plant Annual Flowers & Vines *Flowers picked will last the longest*	**21** Plant Flowering Plants Plant Annual Flowers & Vines *Flowers picked will last the longest*	**22** Plant Flowering Plants Plant Annual Flowers & Vines *Flowers picked will last the longest*	**23** Plant Leafy Greens Prune to Encourage Growth
24 Plant Leafy Greens Prune to Encourage Growth	**25** Plant Fruiting Crops Harvest Crops for Maximum Storage	**26** Plant Fruiting Crops Harvest Crops for Maximum Storage	**27** Plant Root Crops Plant Bulbs	**28** FULL MOON NO GARDENING	**29** Plant Root Crops Plant Bulbs	**30** Plant Flowering Plants Harvest Crops for Maximum Storage

July 2018

Sun	Mon	Tue	Wed	Thu	Fri	Sat
1 Plant Flowering Plants Harvest Crops for Maximum Storage	**2** Plant Flowering Plants Harvest Crops for Maximum Storage	**3** Plant Leafy Greens Transplant for Vigorous Root Growth	**4** Plant Leafy Greens Transplant for Vigorous Root Growth	**5** Plant Fruiting Crops Destroy Weeds	**6** Weeding & Harvesting Destroy Weeds	**7** Weeding & Harvesting Transplant Prune to Limit Growth
8 Weeding & Harvesting Transplant Prune to Limit Growth	**9** Weeding & Harvesting Harvest Herbs & Root Crops	**10** Weeding & Harvesting Harvest Herbs & Root Crops	**11** Weeding & Harvesting Prune to Encourage Growth	**12** NEW MOON NO GARDENING	**13** Plant Leafy Greens Prune to Shape	**14** Plant Fruiting Crops Prune to Shape
15 Plant Fruiting Crops Till – Cultivate Turn Compost	**16** Plant Root Crops Till – Cultivate Turn Compost	**17** Plant Root Crops Till – Cultivate Turn Compost	**18** Plant Flowering Plants Plant Annual Flowers & Vines *Flowers picked will last the longest*	**19** Plant Flowering Plants Plant Annual Flowers & Vines *Flowers picked will last the longest*	**20** Plant Leafy Greens Prune to Encourage Growth	**21** Plant Leafy Greens Prune to Encourage Growth

July 2018

Sun	Mon	Tue	Wed	Thu	Fri	Sat
22 Plant Fruiting Crops Harvest Crops for Maximum Storage	**23** Plant Fruiting Crops Harvest Crops for Maximum Storage	**24** Plant Fruiting Crops Harvest Crops for Maximum Storage	**25** Plant Root Crops Plant Bulbs	**26** Plant Root Crops Plant Bulbs	**27** FULL MOON NO GARDENING	**28** Plant Flowering Plants Harvest Crops for Maximum Storage
29 Plant Flowering Plants Harvest Crops for Maximum Storage	**30** Plant Leafy Greens Plant Annual Flowers & Vines *Flowers picked will last the longest*	**31** Plant Leafy Greens Plant Annual Flowers & Vines *Flowers picked will last the longest*				

August 2018

Sun	Mon	Tue	Wed	Thu	Fri	Sat
			1 Plant Fruiting Crops / Destroy Weeds	**2** Plant Fruiting Crops / Destroy Weeds	**3** Plant Fruiting Crops / Destroy Weeds	**4** Weeding & Harvesting / Transplant / Prune to Limit Growth
5 Weeding & Harvesting / Transplant / Prune to Limit Growth	**6** Weeding & Harvesting / Harvest Herbs & Root Crops	**7** Weeding & Harvesting / Harvest Herbs & Root Crops	**8** Weeding & Harvesting / Prune to Encourage Growth	**9** Weeding & Harvesting / Prune to Encourage Growth	**10** Weeding & Harvesting / Prune to Shape	**11** NEW MOON / NO GARDENING
12 Plant Fruiting Crops / Prune to Shape	**13** Plant Root Crops / Till – Cultivate / Turn Compost	**14** Plant Flowering Plants / Plant Annual Flowers & Vines / *Flowers picked will last the longest*	**15** Plant Flowering Plants / Plant Annual Flowers & Vines / *Flowers picked will last the longest*	**16** Plant Leafy Greens / Prune to Encourage Growth	**17** Plant Leafy Greens / Prune to Encourage Growth	**18** Plant Leafy Greens / Prune to Encourage Growth

August 2018

Sun	Mon	Tue	Wed	Thu	Fri	Sat
19 Plant Fruiting Crops Harvest Crops for Maximum Storage	**20** Plant Fruiting Crops Harvest Crops for Maximum Storage	**21** Plant Root Crops Plant Bulbs	**22** Plant Root Crops Plant Bulbs	**23** Plant Root Crops Plant Bulbs	**24** Plant Flowering Plants Harvest Crops for Maximum Storage	**25** Plant Flowering Plants Harvest Crops for Maximum Storage
26 FULL MOON NO GARDENING	**27** Plant Leafy Greens Transplant for Vigorous Root Growth	**28** Plant Leafy Greens Transplant for Vigorous Root Growth	**29** Plant Fruiting Crops Destroy Weeds	**30** Plant Fruiting Crops Destroy Weeds	**31** Plant Root Crops Transplant Prune to Limit Growth	

September 2018

Sun	Mon	Tue	Wed	Thu	Fri	Sat
						1 Plant Root Crops / Transplant / Prune to Limit Growth
2 Weeding & Harvesting / Harvest Herbs & Root Crops	**3** Weeding & Harvesting / Harvest Herbs & Root Crops	**4** Weeding & Harvesting / Prune to Encourage Growth	**5** Weeding & Harvesting / Prune to Encourage Growth	**6** Weeding & Harvesting / Prune to Shape	**7** Weeding & Harvesting / Prune to Shape	**8** Weeding & Harvesting / Till – Cultivate Turn Compost
9 NEW MOON / NO GARDENING	**10** Plant Flowering Plants / Plant Annual Flowers & Vines / *Flowers picked will last the longest*	**11** Plant Flowering Plants / Plant Annual Flowers & Vines / *Flowers picked will last the longest*	**12** Plant Flowering Plants / Plant Annual Flowers & Vines / *Flowers picked will last the longest*	**13** Plant Leafy Greens / Prune to Encourage Growth	**14** Plant Leafy Greens / Prune to Encourage Growth	**15** Plant Fruiting Crops / Harvest Crops for Maximum Storage

September 2018

Sun	Mon	Tue	Wed	Thu	Fri	Sat
16 Plant Fruiting Crops Harvest Crops for Maximum Storage	**17** Plant Root Crops Plant Bulbs	**18** Plant Root Crops Plant Bulbs	**19** Plant Root Crops Plant Bulbs	**20** Plant Flowering Plants Harvest Crops for Maximum Storage	**21** Plant Flowering Plants Harvest Crops for Maximum Storage	**22** Plant Leafy Greens Transplant for Vigorous Root Growth
23 Plant Leafy Greens Transplant for Vigorous Root Growth	**24** FULL MOON NO GARDENING	**25** Plant Fruiting Crops Destroy Weeds	**26** Plant Fruiting Crops Destroy Weeds	**27** Plant Root Crops Transplant Prune to Limit Growth	**28** Plant Root Crops Transplant Prune to Limit Growth	**29** Plant Flowering Plants Harvest Herbs & Root Crops
30 Plant Flowering Plants Harvest Herbs & Root Crops						

October 2018

Sun	Mon	Tue	Wed	Thu	Fri	Sat
	1 Plant Flowering Plants Harvest Herbs & Root Crops	**2** Weeding & Harvesting Prune to Encourage Growth	**3** Weeding & Harvesting Prune to Encourage Growth	**4** Weeding & Harvesting Prune to Shape	**5** Weeding & Harvesting Prune to Shape	**6** Weeding & Harvesting Till – Cultivate Turn Compost
7 Weeding & Harvesting Till – Cultivate Turn Compost	**8** NEW MOON NO GARDENING	**9** Plant Flowering Plants Plant Annual Flowers & Vines *Flowers picked will last the longest*	**10** Plant Leafy Greens Prune to Encourage Growth	**11** Plant Leafy Greens Prune to Encourage Growth	**12** Plant Fruiting Crops Harvest Crops for Maximum Storage	**13** Plant Fruiting Crops Harvest Crops for Maximum Storage
14 Plant Root Crops Plant Bulbs	**15** Plant Root Crops Plant Bulbs	**16** Plant Root Crops Plant Bulbs	**17** Plant Flowering Plants Harvest Crops for Maximum Storage	**18** Plant Flowering Plants Harvest Crops for Maximum Storage	**19** Plant Flowering Plants Harvest Crops for Maximum Storage	**20** Plant Leafy Greens Transplant for Vigorous Root Growth

October 2018

Sun	Mon	Tue	Wed	Thu	Fri	Sat
21 Plant Leafy Greens / Transplant for Vigorous Root Growth	**22** Plant Fruiting Crops / Destroy Weeds	**23** Plant Fruiting Crops / Destroy Weeds	**24** FULL MOON / NO GARDENING	**25** Plant Root Crops / Transplant / Prune to Limit Growth	**26** Plant Root Crops / Transplant / Prune to Limit Growth	**27** Plant Flowering Plants / Harvest Herbs & Root Crops
28 Plant Flowering Plants / Harvest Herbs & Root Crops	**29** Plant Leafy Greens / Prune to Encourage Growth	**30** Plant Leafy Greens / Prune to Encourage Growth	**31** Weeding & Harvesting / Prune to Shape			

November 2018

Sun	Mon	Tue	Wed	Thu	Fri	Sat
				1 Weeding & Harvesting / Prune to Shape	**2** Weeding & Harvesting / Till – Cultivate Turn Compost	**3** Weeding & Harvesting / Till – Cultivate Turn Compost
4 Weeding & Harvesting / Flowers picked will last the longest	**5** Weeding & Harvesting / Flowers picked will last the longest	**6** Weeding & Harvesting / Prune to Encourage Growth	**7** NEW MOON / NO GARDENING	**8** Plant Leafy Greens / Prune to Encourage Growth	**9** Plant Fruiting Crops / Harvest Crops for Maximum Storage	**10** Plant Fruiting Crops / Harvest Crops for Maximum Storage
11 Plant Root Crops / Plant Bulbs	**12** Plant Root Crops / Plant Bulbs	**13** Plant Flowering Plants / Harvest Crops for Maximum Storage	**14** Plant Flowering Plants / Harvest Crops for Maximum Storage	**15** Plant Flowering Plants / Harvest Crops for Maximum Storage	**16** Plant Leafy Greens / Transplant for Vigorous Root Growth	**17** Plant Leafy Greens / Transplant for Vigorous Root Growth

November 2018

Sun	Mon	Tue	Wed	Thu	Fri	Sat
18 Plant Fruiting Crops / Destroy Weeds	**19** Plant Fruiting Crops / Destroy Weeds	**20** Plant Fruiting Crops / Destroy Weeds	**21** Plant Root Crops / Transplant / Prune to Limit Growth	**22** Plant Root Crops / Transplant / Prune to Limit Growth	**23** FULL MOON / NO GARDENING	**24** Plant Flowering Plants / Harvest Herbs & Root Crops
25 Plant Leafy Greens / Prune to Encourage Growth	**26** Plant Leafy Greens / Prune to Encourage Growth	**27** Plant Fruiting Crops / Prune to Shape	**28** Plant Fruiting Crops / Prune to Shape	**29** Weeding & Harvesting / Till – Cultivate Turn Compost	**30** Weeding & Harvesting / Till – Cultivate Turn Compost	

December 2018

Sun	Mon	Tue	Wed	Thu	Fri	Sat
						1 Weeding & Harvesting Flowers picked will last the longest
2 Weeding & Harvesting Flowers picked will last the longest	**3** Weeding & Harvesting Flowers picked will last the longest	**4** Weeding & Harvesting Prune to Encourage Growth	**5** Weeding & Harvesting Prune to Encourage Growth	**6** Weeding & Harvesting Harvest Crops for Maximum Storage	**7** NEW MOON NO GARDENING	**8** Plant Root Crops Plant Bulbs
9 Plant Root Crops Plant Bulbs	**10** Plant Root Crops Plant Bulbs	**11** Plant Flowering Plants Harvest Crops for Maximum Storage	**12** Plant Flowering Plants Harvest Crops for Maximum Storage	**13** Plant Leafy Greens Transplant for Vigorous Root Growth	**14** Plant Leafy Greens Transplant for Vigorous Root Growth	**15** Plant Leafy Greens Transplant for Vigorous Root Growth

December 2018

Sun	Mon	Tue	Wed	Thu	Fri	Sat
16 Plant Fruiting Crops Destroy Weeds	**17** Plant Fruiting Crops Destroy Weeds	**18** Plant Root Crops Transplant Prune to Limit Growth	**19** Plant Root Crops Transplant Prune to Limit Growth	**20** Plant Flowering Plants Harvest Herbs & Root Crops	**21** Plant Flowering Plants Harvest Herbs & Root Crops	**22** FULL MOON NO GARDENING
23 Plant Leafy Greens Prune to Encourage Growth Flowers picked will last the longest	**24** Plant Fruiting Crops Prune to Shape	**25** Plant Fruiting Crops Prune to Shape	**26** Plant Fruiting Crops Prune to Shape	**27** Plant Root Crops Till – Cultivate Turn Compost	**28** Plant Root Crops Till – Cultivate Turn Compost	**29** Weeding & Harvesting Flowers picked will last the longest
30 Weeding & Harvesting Flowers picked will last the longest	**31** Weeding & Harvesting Prune to Encourage Growth					

January 2019

Sun	Mon	Tue	Wed	Thu	Fri	Sat
		1 Weeding & Harvesting / Prune to Encourage Growth	**2** Weeding & Harvesting / Harvest Crops for Maximum Storage	**3** Weeding & Harvesting / Harvest Crops for Maximum Storage	**4** Weeding & Harvesting / Harvest Crops for Maximum Storage	**5** NEW MOON / NO GARDENING
6 Plant Root Crops / Plant Bulbs	**7** Plant Flowering Plants / Harvest Crops for Maximum Storage	**8** Plant Flowering Plants / Harvest Crops for Maximum Storage	**9** Plant Flowering Plants / Harvest Crops for Maximum Storage	**10** Plant Leafy Greens / Transplant for Vigorous Root Growth	**11** Plant Leafy Greens / Transplant for Vigorous Root Growth	**12** Plant Fruiting Crops / Destroy Weeds
13 Plant Fruiting Crops / Destroy Weeds	**14** Plant Fruiting Crops / Destroy Weeds	**15** Plant Root Crops / Transplant / Prune to Limit Growth	**16** Plant Root Crops / Transplant / Prune to Limit Growth	**17** Plant Flowering Plants / Harvest Herbs & Root Crops	**18** Plant Flowering Plants / Harvest Herbs & Root Crops	**19** Plant Leafy Greens / Prune to Encourage Growth

January 2019

Sun	Mon	Tue	Wed	Thu	Fri	Sat
20 Plant Leafy Greens Prune to Encourage Growth	**21** FULL MOON NO GARDENING	**22** Plant Fruiting Crops Prune to Shape	**23** Plant Root Crops Till – Cultivate Turn Compost	**24** Plant Root Crops Till – Cultivate Turn Compost	**25** Plant Flowering Plants Plant Annual Flowers & Vines *Flowers picked will last the longest*	**26** Plant Flowering Plants Plant Annual Flowers & Vines *Flowers picked will last the longest*
27 Weeding & Harvesting Prune to Encourage Growth	**28** Weeding & Harvesting Prune to Encourage Growth	**29** Weeding & Harvesting Harvest Crops for Maximum Storage	**30** Weeding & Harvesting Harvest Crops for Maximum Storage	**31** Weeding & Harvesting Harvest Crops for Maximum Storage		

February 2019

Sun	Mon	Tue	Wed	Thu	Fri	Sat
					1 Weeding & Harvesting, Plant Bulbs	**2** Weeding & Harvesting, Plant Bulbs
3 Weeding & Harvesting, Harvest Crops for Maximum Storage	**4** NEW MOON, NO GARDENING	**5** Plant Flowering Plants, Harvest Crops for Maximum Storage	**6** Plant Leafy Greens, Transplant for Vigorous Root Growth	**7** Plant Leafy Greens, Transplant for Vigorous Root Growth	**8** Plant Fruiting Crops, Destroy Weeds	**9** Plant Fruiting Crops, Destroy Weeds
10 Plant Fruiting Crops, Destroy Weeds	**11** Plant Root Crops, Transplant, Prune to Limit Growth	**12** Plant Root Crops, Transplant, Prune to Limit Growth	**13** Plant Flowering Plants, Harvest Herbs & Root Crops	**14** Plant Flowering Plants, Harvest Herbs & Root Crops	**15** Plant Leafy Greens, Prune to Encourage Growth	**16** Plant Leafy Greens, Prune to Encourage Growth

February 2019

Sun	Mon	Tue	Wed	Thu	Fri	Sat
17 Plant Fruiting Crops Prune to Shape	**18** Plant Fruiting Crops Prune to Shape	**19** FULL MOON NO GARDENING	**20** Plant Root Crops Till – Cultivate Turn Compost	**21** Plant Flowering Plants Plant Annual Flowers & Vines *Flowers picked will last the longest*	**22** Plant Flowering Plants Plant Annual Flowers & Vines *Flowers picked will last the longest*	**23** Plant Leafy Greens Prune to Encourage Growth
24 Plant Leafy Greens Prune to Encourage Growth	**25** Plant Leafy Greens Prune to Encourage Growth	**26** Weeding & Harvesting Harvest Crops for Maximum Storage	**27** Weeding & Harvesting Harvest Crops for Maximum Storage	**28** Weeding & Harvesting Plant Bulbs		

March 2019

Sun	Mon	Tue	Wed	Thu	Fri	Sat
					1 Weeding & Harvesting Plant Bulbs	**2** Weeding & Harvesting Plant Bulbs
3 Weeding & Harvesting Harvest Crops for Maximum Storage	**4** Weeding & Harvesting Harvest Crops for Maximum Storage	**5** Weeding & Harvesting Transplant for Vigorous Root Growth	**6** NEW MOON NO GARDENING	**7** Plant Leafy Greens Transplant for Vigorous Root Growth	**8** Plant Fruiting Crops Destroy Weeds	**9** Plant Fruiting Crops Destroy Weeds
10 Plant Root Crops Transplant Prune to Limit Growth	**11** Plant Root Crops Transplant Prune to Limit Growth	**12** Plant Flowering Plants Harvest Herbs & Root Crops	**13** Plant Flowering Plants Harvest Herbs & Root Crops	**14** Plant Flowering Plants Harvest Herbs & Root Crops	**15** Plant Leafy Greens Prune to Encourage Growth	**16** Plant Leafy Greens Prune to Encourage Growth

March 2019

Sun	Mon	Tue	Wed	Thu	Fri	Sat
17 Plant Fruiting Crops Prune to Shape	**18** Plant Fruiting Crops Prune to Shape	**19** Plant Root Crops Till – Cultivate Turn Compost	**20** FULL MOON NO GARDENING	**21** Plant Flowering Plants Plant Annual Flowers & Vines *Flowers picked will last the longest*	**22** Plant Flowering Plants Plant Annual Flowers & Vines *Flowers picked will last the longest*	**23** Plant Leafy Greens Prune to Encourage Growth
24 Plant Leafy Greens Prune to Encourage Growth Harvest Crops for Maximum Storage	**25** Plant Fruiting Crops Harvest Crops for Maximum Storage	**26** Plant Fruiting Crops Harvest Crops for Maximum Storage	**27** Plant Root Crops Plant Bulbs	**28** Weeding & Harvesting Plant Bulbs	**29** Weeding & Harvesting Plant Bulbs	**30** Weeding & Harvesting Harvest Crops for Maximum Storage
31 Weeding & Harvesting Harvest Crops for Maximum Storage						

MY PLANTING RECORD

DESCRIPTION of VEGETABLE FLOWER	When Planted	Moon Phase	Sign	1st Harvest	Last Harvest
PLANT PRUNED	When Pruned	Moon Phase	Sign	Purpose? to Shape; Stimulate Growth; Retard Growth	

MY PLANTING RECORD

DESCRIPTION of VEGETABLE FLOWER	When Planted	Moon Phase	Sign	1st Harvest	Last Harvest

PLANT PRUNED	When Pruned	Moon Phase	Sign	Purpose? to Shape; Stimulate Growth; Retard Growth

Companion Planting

Look deep into nature and you will understand
everything better. Albert Einstein

On a final note, something to consider: companion planting. It's too large of a topic to cover, here but I want to give you an idea of its importance. Think of your garden as a community. Some plants excrete that which is toxic to other plants. Following the characteristics of nature, there are plants that are compatible with some plants and not with others. For example, Calendula, or pot marigolds, is a companion to carrots. Why? The scent given off the marigolds covers the scent of the carrot so the carrot flies don't know where to find them. I think that is so cool. Scented geraniums do the same thing when planted next to parsnips. Oregano plants deter pests in general

Tomato and dill make a delicious salad but don't grow them together. When the dill plant matures, it attracts the hornworm which is detrimental to the tomato plant.

Some plants are companions as they exchange nutrients in the soil. What one plant gives off another plant uses. So if a plant doesn't like or can't handle a particular nutrient, such as alkaline plants don't do well with acid ph, they will not grow well.

Radishes are traditionally difficult plants to grow. Maybe so, but if

Herb ~ Sense

Fertilizing herbs result in lush green leaves. They may look lush and beautiful, but the herbs then have little flavor. For that reason herbs do better with NO fertilizing. Do your own test and prove it for yourself.

Harvest your herbs frequently to promote growth - it's a natural way of pruning.

radishes are planted with a companion plant, they grow very well. Not only do radishes love cucumber plants, the radish also repels the cucumber beetle. These concepts of companion planting are all ones that I have successfully tried (plus many more).

Speaking of cucumbers, for a few years, I had trouble with the cucumbers developing a powdery mildew which quickly killed the plant. As I didn't want to use fungicides on the plant, I struggled for many years. Finally, I found the perfect solution! Horsetail tea. I make the mixture, (see below) and began to spray the cucumber leaves when they were young. The horsetail tea builds the immune system to the powdery mildew spores which are airborne and I haven't had the problem ever since. I haven't tried this as I don't have this problem, but I heard that horsetail tea works on peach leaf curl as well.

Horsetail Tea
(Equisetum arvense)

In a glass mix 1/8 cup of dried leaves in 1 gallon of un-chlorinated water. Bring to a boil, then let simmer for at least 1-1/2 hour. Cool and strain.

Store extra concentrate in a glass container which will keep for a month.

Dilute this mix, adding 5-10 parts of un-chlorinated water to one part concentrate.

Begin to spray when plant is young, to build its' immune system, Once a week. Spray the leave on the outside and the underside.

Spray plants leaves that show any symptoms of fungal type disease once every 4 days. If it rains, spray after the rain.

When the pioneers arrived in America in the 1600's, the Iroquois Indians taught farmers the principle of the "three sisters" The Iroquois grew corn, squash and beans together. The corn stocks supported the vines of the beans while the squash provided shade for the corn and beans as well as minimizing the growth of weeds.

• Plant the corn after all threat of frost is gone

- Plant the pole beans when corn is 5" tall
- Plant the squash 1 week later

Another benefit: small animals were deterred from the crop as they didn't like to step on the squash leaves. This method is still practiced in gardening today and is referred to as the "Three Sisters Method" of planting.

Those pesky whiteflies have attacked my tomatoes plants. I have found that they can be controlled by planting Nasturtium by the tomato plant. You might also check the soil composition as it may be lacking phosphorus or magnesium. I personally don't check the soil composition, I just make certain that the fertilizer I use contains phosphorus or magnesium. Whiteflies attach to the tomato plant when it is vulnerable with a mineral deficiency.

What is most important is to have fun and garden with a Light Heart. Energy follows thought, so, where your attention is while gardening will radiate from the plants in terms of beauty and nutrition. ENJOY!

References

bachbiodynamics.com/planting-calendar-research.html

Carrots Love Tomatoes by Louise Riotte 1998 Storey Publishing, LLC, North Adams MA

nationalgeographic.com (search gardening)

The American Ephemeris for the 21st Century, 2000-2050 at Midnight, by Neil F. Michelsen ACS Publications, New Hampshire

The Old Farmer's Almanac, by Yankee Publishing Incorporated Dublin NH

Notes

Notes

Notes

Notes

Notes

Notes

Notes

Notes

Notes

Notes

Notes

Notes

Printed in the United States
By Bookmasters